PIANO

Listen & Learn

HOMESPUN MUSIC INSTRUCTION

David Bennett
COHEN
TEACHES
Rock 'n' Roll Piano

A Hands-on
Beginner's Course
in Traditional
Rock Styles

T0052552

ISBN 0-634-06221-2

HOMESPUN *Tapes*

EXCLUSIVELY DISTRIBUTED BY

HAL•LEONARD®
CORPORATION

7777 W. BLUEMOUND RD. P.O. BOX 13819 MILWAUKEE, WI 53213

© 2003 HOMESPUN TAPES LTD.
BOX 340
WOODSTOCK, NY 12498-0694
All Rights Reserved

Visit Hal Leonard Online at
www.halleonard.com

PIANO *Listen & Learn*
HOMESPUN MUSIC INSTRUCTION

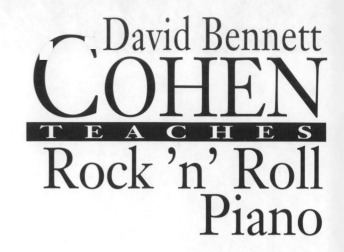

David Bennett
COHEN
T E A C H E S
Rock 'n' Roll Piano

A Hands-on
Beginner's Course
in Traditional
Rock Styles

Table of Contents

CD instruction makes it easy! Find the section of the lesson you want with the press of a finger; play that segment over and over until you've mastered it; easily skip over parts you've already mastered—no clumsy rewinding or fast forwarding to find your spot; listen with the best possible audio fidelity; follow along track-by-track with the book.

Introduction

The piano has a long and illustrious history in rock and roll music, both in a supporting rhythm role and as a lead instrument. My goal in writing this book is to try and put those roles into perspective by paraphrasing the great rock piano pioneers of the '50s and '60s. Using my explanations and examples, you should be able to take their ideas and expand on them, working towards the ultimate goal of developing your own style.

Music has an evolutionary aspect to it: everything is based on something that came before. Like many of us, I grew up learning classical piano but I didn't enjoy my lessons. It wasn't until I heard the piano used in a different context that I really got turned on to the instrument. I suspect many of you had similar experiences. My classical background stayed with me, though, and it influences the music that I play today.

I cover two types of rock piano techniques in this collection: soloing, which mostly follows the blues scale, and rhythm, which can be based either on simple repetition or on more complex rhythmic patterns.

When playing rhythm, what you are looking for is the "drive" that makes you tap your feet, dance or just plain move to the music. In a band you'll be part of the rhythm section, playing with others as an ensemble. There is a beautiful unity that occurs when the rhythm section is working together to make the lead instrument sound better. When the band is playing at its best it becomes another instrument; if it's a four-piece group, then the band itself becomes virtually the fifth instrument.

When playing in a band the treble notes can sometimes conflict with the saxophone, guitar, harmonica, vocal or other lead instruments, so be aware of this. Stay away, too, from the very low bass notes. The bass player listens down there, and if he hears something that he's not playing it can confuse the music. Sometimes the piano and bass play the same bass line, which can set up a churning rhythmic sound that's irresistible.

Although there are many rock players who only use their right hand, I think it's best to use both hands. One-hand playing might be appropriate during certain solos, but there are syncopations that you can only get with both hands that can really drive the music. Just try and stay out of the way of the other instruments, and you should be fine.

In the early days of recording, the engineers and producers would put a single microphone in the room and record the band live. One or another of the instruments would get buried, and it was often the piano. During recording and live performance, the piano would invariably get lost so many piano players developed a somewhat "busy" style. They were used to not being heard anyway, and this just compounded the problem. Nowadays, with all of the instruments isolated and the possibility of overdubbing, the style has modified itself. Still, many piano players play that "busy" style. Sometimes it's appropriate, but often it's not. One of the most important pieces of advice that I can give any aspiring piano player is to listen carefully to the music and play what seems most appropriate.

Even though I demonstrate the various examples in either C or G, because these keys are easy tounderstand, you really should be able to play in all of the keys. Even though there are different fingering patterns to each of the various keys, this simply has to be mastered

As always, the best way to learn this music is to listen to as many piano players as possible. The list is almost endless, but I would like to mention Johnnie Johnson, Little Richard, Fats Domino and Jerry Lee Lewis as a place to start.

Finally, I would like to say that there is nothing better than to hear a piano in a rock band. I hope this book and CD will help get you started playing this great American music.

David Bennett Cohen

Fast Funk/Eighth Note Rhythm

② Major Scale

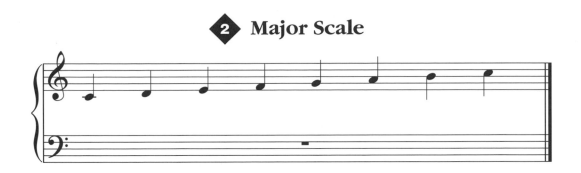

③ Chord Numbering

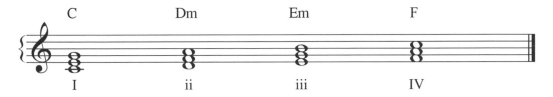

Chuck Berry Rhythm

Rock 'n' Roll Rhythm

④ "Little Richard" Style - Explained

Blues

Turnaround

6 Glissando - Explained

7 Glisssando - Demonstrated

8 Glissando - Variations

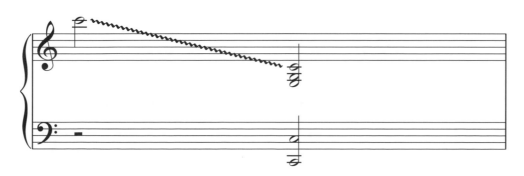

9 Glissandos Used in a Verse

Blues Verse End

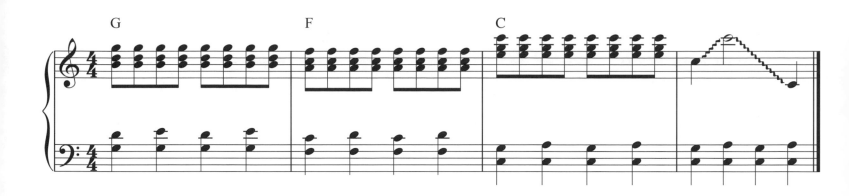

🔟 Blues Scale Uses in Solos

Blues Solo

Blues Scale Variation

♦11 Solo Using Various Ideas

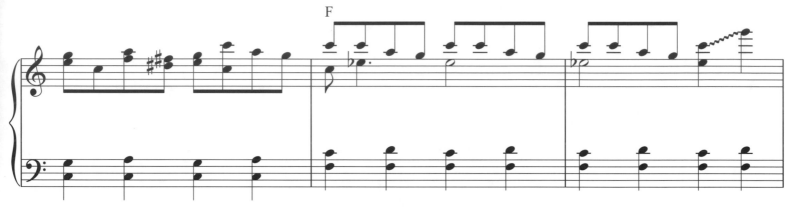

13 Chord Clusters - Explained

14 Chord Clusters - Played

◆16 Using Triplets in the Right Hand

◆17 "Little Richard" Style Bass Line

◆18 Bass Line with Right Hand 1/8 (eighth) Notes

◆19 Bass Line with Right Hand Variations

Variation 2

Variation 3

Variation 4

Variation 5

14

"Bo Diddley" Rhythm

24 12 Bar Blues Progression

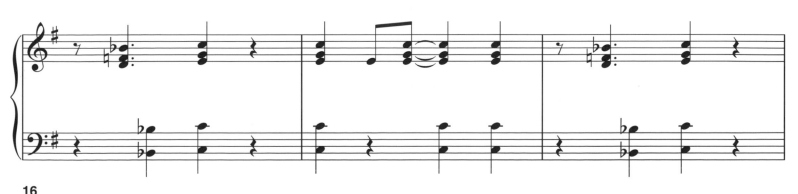

26 Using Chords in the Left Hand

27 Phrases for Soloing

Rock 'n' Roll Ballad

28 I-VI-II-V Progression with Triplets in Right Hand

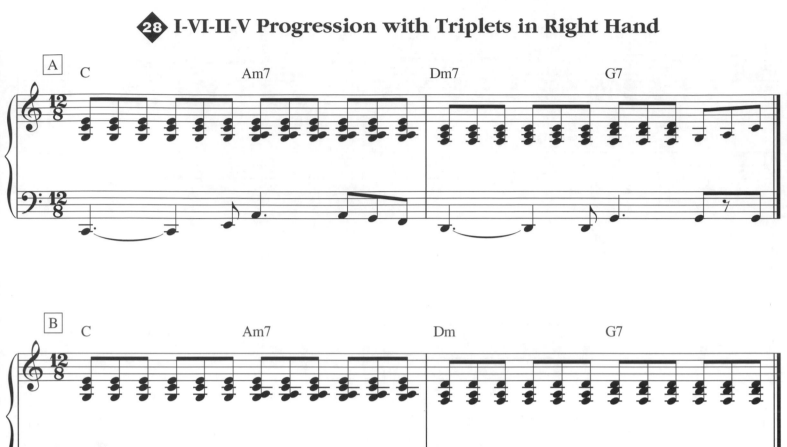

29 Using Chords in Left Hand

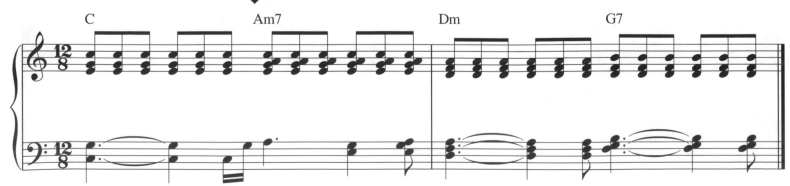

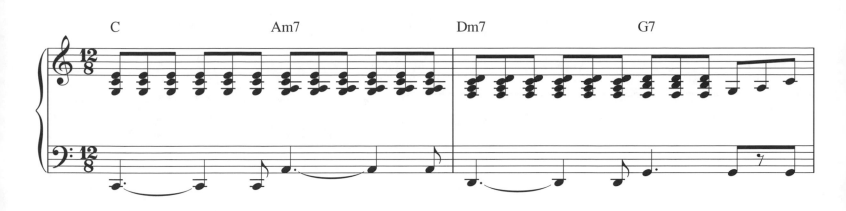

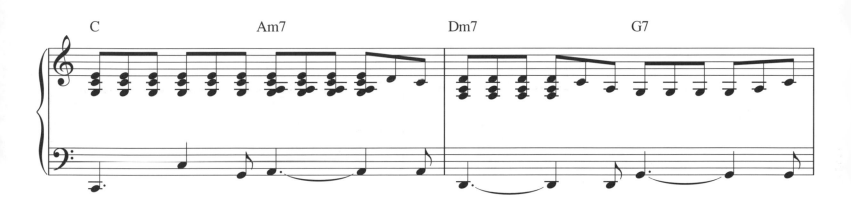

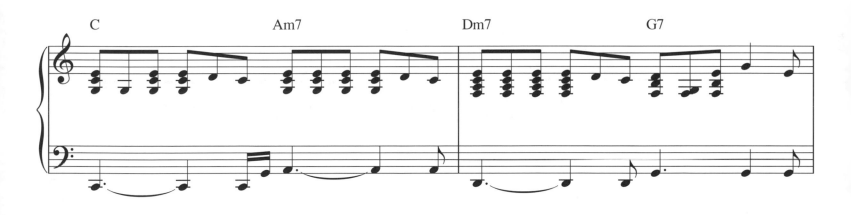

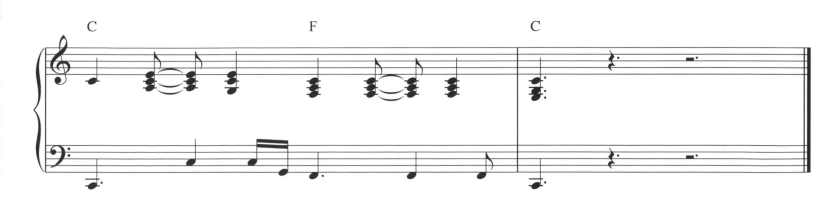

31 ▸ Bridge Chords

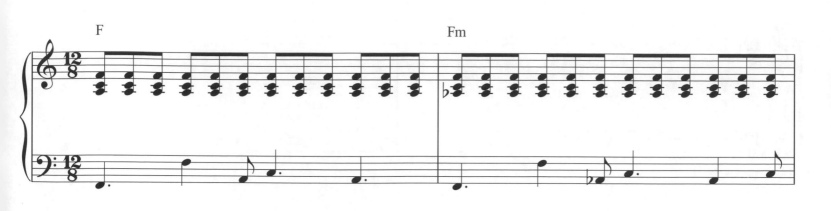

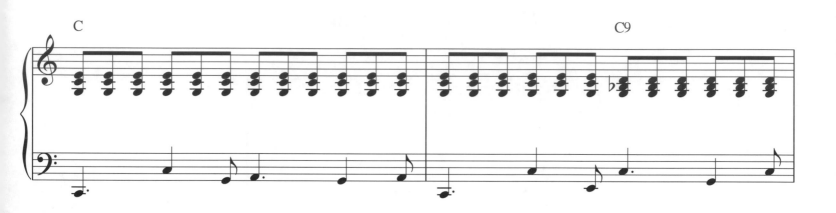

Alternate Ending

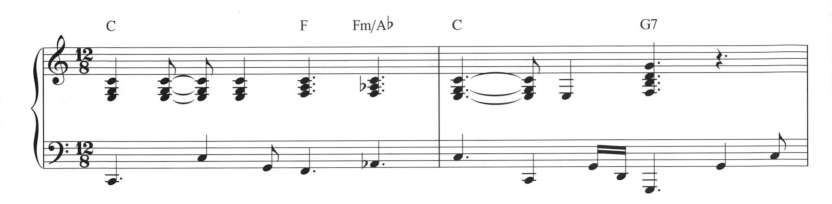

32 Chord Substitutions

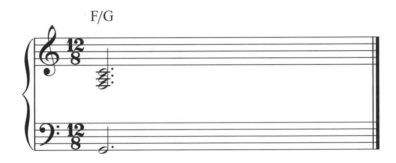

F/G In Context

33 Whole Form Played

Solo Using Minor 3rd

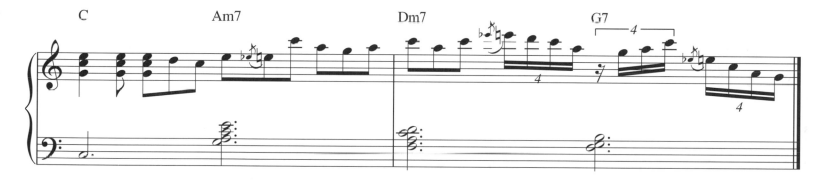

"Fats Domino" Rhythm

35 Demonstrated

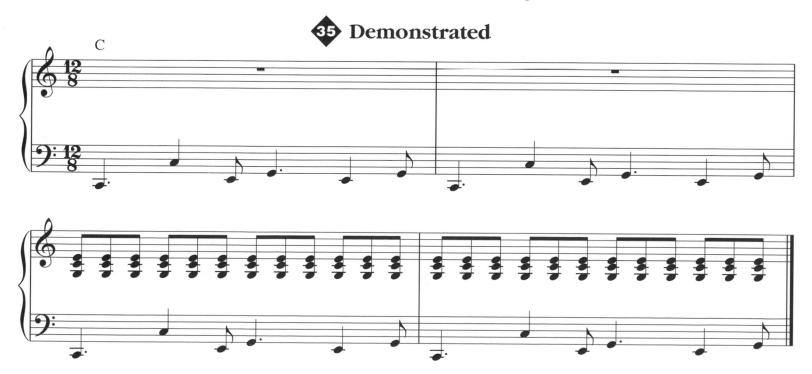

36 8 Bar Blues Progression

Turnaround

Turnaround Demonstrated

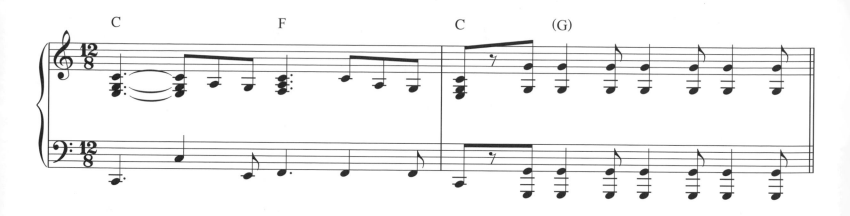

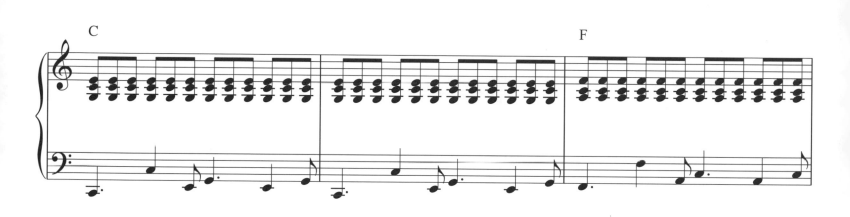

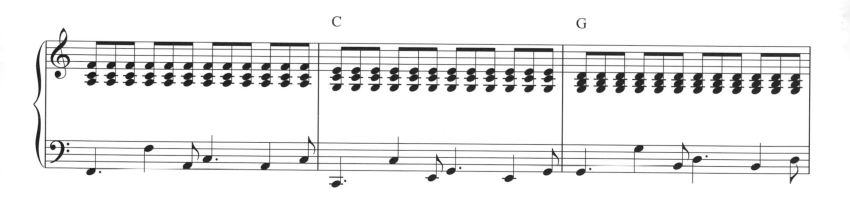

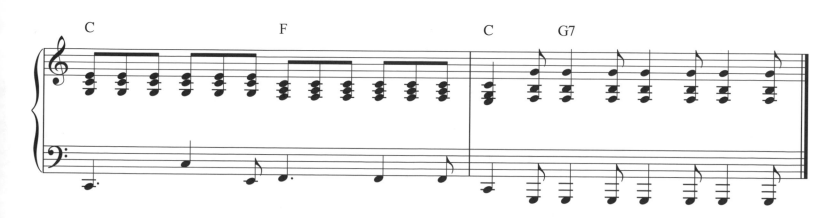

37 Up-tempo Rhythm

38 Rhythm Piano Concepts

39 Rock 'n' Roll Arrangements

Auld Lang Syne

Rock 'n' Roll Ballad

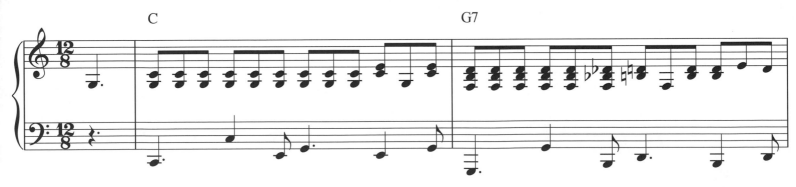

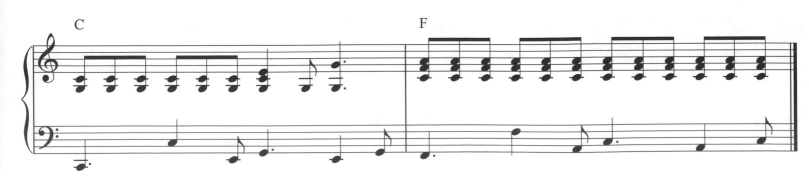

Eighth Note Rhythm

40 Two Chord Progressions

Stop Time Rhythms

32

43 Variations

Ex. 1

Ex. 2

Ex. 3

Stop Time with Solo Ex. 2

Ex. 2

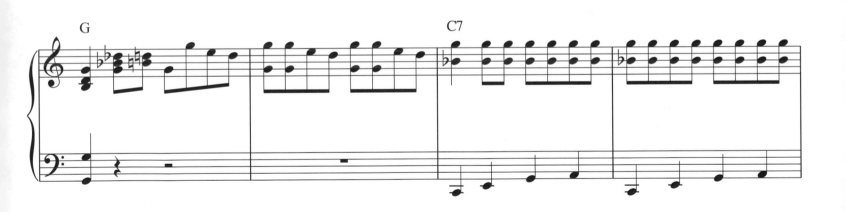

◆45 Using Arpeggios

Rock 'n' Roll Shuffle

48 ◆ **Played in the Key of C**

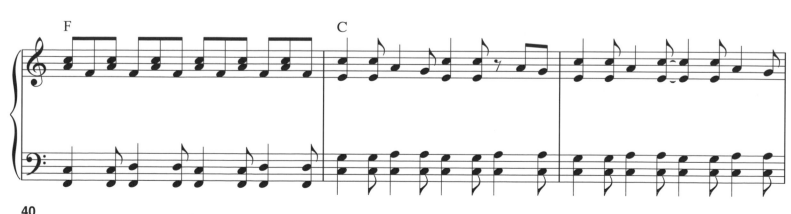

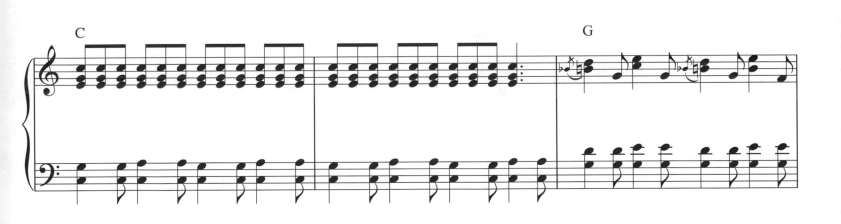

 49 Broken Down

LH with Counting

One, two, three   Two, two, three   Three, two, three   Four, two, three

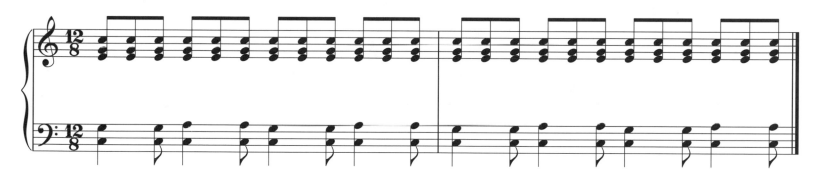

Both Hands

Single Note Triplets

"Tied" Triplets

42

50 Played with Variations

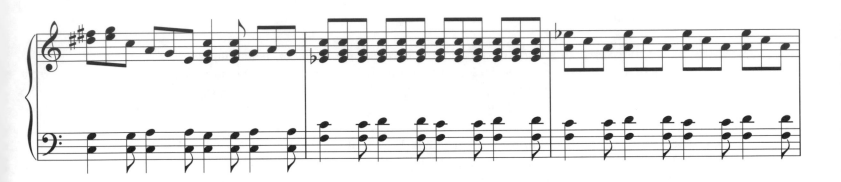

Biography

"Mr. Cohen isn't the average hippie gone Wall Street. He's also a certifiably smokin' barrel-house rhumba boogie-woogie piano player in the James Booker/Professor Longhair/Dr. John vein."

David Bennett Cohen has been a professional musician for more than 25 years. Best known for his innovative keyboard playing as an original member of the '60s rock band, Country Joe and the Fish, he is an equally accomplished guitar player who has been involved in numerous music scenes throughout his varied career.

David began his musical education at the age of seven, studying classical piano for seven years. While studying the piano, he began to teach himself the guitar, beginning at the age of nine. When he was 14, he heard boogie-woogie piano for the first time and was hooked. Since then he has explored many different styles of blues and popular music. He was fortunate enough to have heard Otis Spann, Professor Longhair, Meade Lux Lewis and other masters of the genre perform live.

"What separates Cohen from a lot of other players is his unassuming ease behind the keys, and the ability to take that admiration past rote emulation, invoking the spirits of boogie-woogie, stride and blues piano greats without ever forcing things or just replicating other folks' licks."

Over the years, he as played and/or recorded with The Blues Project, Mick Taylor, The Luther Tucker Blues Band, Elvin Bishop, Melvin Van Peebles, Happy and Artie Traum, Arlen Roth, Eric Andersen, David Blue, Tim Hardin, Norton Buffalo, Jerry Miller (of Moby Grape), Steve Miller, Jimi Hendrix, Johnnie Winter, John Cippolina, Huey Lewis, Michael Bloomfield, Bob Weir, John Kahn and others.

As a solo performer, he has shared the bill with Country Joe McDonald, Kenny Rankin, Bonnie Raitt, Richard Thompson, Jerry Garcia, Leo Kottke, Rufus Thomas, Meatloaf, Booker T., The Roaches, Kingfish and many others.

David has recorded two audio teaching tapes series (*Blues/Rock, Piano* and *Ragtime Piano*) and a three-video tape series (*Blues Piano*) for Homespun Tapes. In addition, he has released two guitar instruction albums for Kicking Mule Records.

For the past several years, David has been busy composing, writing songs, teaching piano and guitar, performing and recording. He plays around the New York area with his own band, Crawfish Royale, and a Tex-Mex Country band (The Plumbers). Upcoming projects include dual piano recordings with Tom Constanten (keyboardist of The Grateful Dead from 1967 to 1970, Relix Records) and two others with Pete Sears (from Jefferson Starship) and Howie Wyeth.

"Cohen radiates the 88's impeccably."
All quotes from *CMJ New Music Report*

A Selected Discography

Country Joe and the Fish:

Electric Music for the Mind and Body	Vanguard Records VRS-9244
I Feel Like I'm Fixin' to Die	Vanguard Records VSD-79266
Together	Vanguard Records VSD-79277
Here We Are Again	Vanguard Records
Greatest Hits	Vanguard Records VSD-6545
Reunion	Fantasy Records F-9530

Other Recordings:

Blues Project	Capitol Records SMAS-11017
David Bennett Cohen — The Connection	Bullseye Records B8442-1
David Bennett Cohen at the Piano	Ray Baby Records RB-1022
Brian Kramer and the Blues Masters–Win or Lose	Monsoon Records FVCC-4862

Instructional Tapes:

Blues/Rock Piano, six audio-tape series	Homespun Tapes
Blues/Rock, Piano Practice Tape, one audio tape	Homespun Tapes
Ragtime Piano, six audio-tape series	Homespun Tapes
Blues Piano, three-video set	Homespun Tapes
How to Play Folk Guitar	Kicking Mule Records
Rock 'n' Roll Guitar	Kicking Mule Records

LISTEN & LEARN SERIES

This exciting new series features lessons from the top pros with in-depth CD instruction and thorough accompanying book.

GUITAR

**Russ Barenberg Teaches
Twenty Bluegrass Guitar Solos**
00695220 Book/CD Pack $19.95

**Keola Beamer Teaches
Hawaiian Slack Key Guitar**
00695338 Book/CD Pack $19.95

**Rory Block Teaches
Classics of Country Blues Guitar**
00699065 Book/CD Pack $19.95

**Roy's Blues Book – Songs & Guitar
Arrangements of Roy Book Binder**
00695808 Book/CD Pack $19.95

**Cathy Fink and Marcy Marxer's
Kids' Guitar Songbook**
00699258 Book/CD Pack $14.95

The Guitar of Jorma Kaukonen
00695184 Book/CD Pack $19.95

Tony Rice Teaches Bluegrass Guitar
00695045 Book/CD Pack $19.95

**Artie Traum Teaches
Essential Blues for Acoustic Guitar**
00695805 Book/CD Pack $19.95

**Artie Traum Teaches Essential Chords
& Progressions for Acoustic Guitar**
00695259 Book/CD Pack $14.95

**Artie Traum Teaches
101 Essential Riffs for Acoustic Guitar**
00695260 Book/CD Pack $14.95

Happy Traum Teaches Blues Guitar
00841082 Book/CD Pack $19.95

**Richard Thompson Teaches
Traditional Guitar Instrumentals**
00841083 Book/CD Pack $19.95

BANJO

**Tony Trischka Teaches
20 Easy Banjo Solos**
00699056 Book/CD Pack $19.95

MANDOLIN

**Sam Bush Teaches
Bluegrass Mandolin Repertoire**
00695339 Book/CD Pack $19.95

HARMONICA

**Paul Butterfield Teaches
Blues Harmonica**
00699089 Book/CD Pack $19.95

**John Sebastian Teaches
Blues Harmonica**
00841074 Book/CD Pack $19.95

PIANO

**David Bennett Cohen Teaches
Blues Piano**
A Hands-On Course in Traditional Blues Piano
00841084 Volume 1 Book/CD Pack...................$19.95
00290498 Volume 2 Book/CD Pack...................$19.95

Warren Bernhardt Teaches Jazz Piano
00699062 Volume 1 Book/CD Pack $19.95
00699084 Volume 2 Book/CD Pack $19.95

Dr. John Teaches New Orleans Piano
00699090 Volume 1 Book/CD Pack $19.95
00699093 Volume 2 Book/CD Pack $19.95
00699094 Volume 3 Book/CD Pack $19.95

PENNYWHISTLE

**Cathal McConnell Teaches
Irish Pennywhistle**
00841081 Book/CD Pack $19.95

FOR MORE INFORMATION, SEE YOUR LOCAL MUSIC DEALER,
OR WRITE TO:

HAL•LEONARD® CORPORATION
7777 W. BLUEMOUND RD. P.O. BOX 13819 MILWAUKEE, WI 53213

Visit Hal Leonard online at
www.halleonard.com

Prices and availability subject to change without notice.

1203